iNeverWorry

Derrick "DB" Bedford

Fourth Edition, June 2018

Copyright © 2018 Derrick "DB" Bedford

Cover Design: Stacey Debono/Stacey Debono Photography and Graphic Design

Edited by Stacey Debono

ISBN: 1514341786

ISBN-13: 978-1514341780

DEDICATION

This book is dedicated to my grandparents, Spencer and Gertrude Bedford, who both transitioned from this earth before they had a chance to witness their legacy come to fruition.

3

Contents

iNEVERWORRY 7

MIND YOUR BUSINESS..13

MANAGING YOUR REACTIONS.......................................23

USING YOUR SPIDEY SENSES..31

MANAGING RELATIONSHIPS 39

TEMPERAMENT THEORY..47

THE ORGANIZER..51

THE PEACEFUL SPIRIT..55

THE ANALYZER..59

THE CREATIVE SPIRIT..63

MOODS & ATTITUDES...67

PATIENCE..75

ACKNOWLEDGMENTS..79

ABOUT THE AUTHOR 85

1

iNEVERWORRY

Just because you have a nightmare doesn't mean you stop dreaming. - Jill Scott

Never Worry is an idea that came to me as a t-shirt concept back in 1995 while I was hanging in my community of Brookfield Village in Oakland, CA. The brand was created during a time in my life when every day was a struggle and just surviving throughout the day equated to some level of success. My brother Darrin and my buddy Nardo played a significant role in breathing life into the original concept of *Never Worry Stress Free Clothing*, which eventually evolved into iNeverWorry Consulting & Training.

My homie, Rod Campbell (DopeOnly and OaklandUSA creator), pitched the idea of putting the lower case "i" in front of *Never Worry* as an innovative way to revolutionize the way we market the brand. Although *Never Worry* was created during a time in my life that was complicated with challenges, I always understood the importance of maintaining a positive and healthy mindset.

Over the years something that was a t-shirt being sold on the street corner evolved into a powerful platform that showed people how to manage emotions through training/seminars, literature and merchandising.

Growing up in the city of Oakland I stayed in trouble, getting arrested multiple times between the ages of thirteen and twenty-three. My life was full of criminal activity that certainly had an impact on the crime rate in my community. I hustled in the streets during a time when money was plentiful and getting arrested didn't matter because you could simply bail out and fight your case from the streets. Most of the time I would get my probation extended and I would be comfortable with that since all my homeboys at the time were on probation. It just didn't seem abnormal.

Like most things in life, there comes a time when you have to change and make adjustments in order to grow. My turning point in life took place in the Alameda County Superior Courthouse while standing in front of the Honorable Judge Larry Goodman facing charges for attempting to take another man's life. To this day we debate how many times I stood in front of him facing charges; the only thing we can agree on is that it was more than once.

We all have heard the saying, "Hindsight is 20/20", and as I reflect back, Judge Goodman was the first person that I remember exercising emotional intelligence from a professional standpoint. Despite my reputation in the streets and constantly ending up in his courtroom for a variety of offenses, he took the time to recognize my potential before I even understood that I had it.

So let's put this in perspective: Judge Goodman sits on the bench every day and listens to countless individuals defend their actions or wrong doings in his courtroom. Some defenses are valid, but it would be safe to say that most were not. He has given plenty of people a chance to do right, only to have them come back in front of him with even more serious charges. During his work day he certainly must cycle through a range of emotions such as frustration, anger and disappointment while listening to the details of multiple criminal cases. But somehow he was able to set his feelings aside and recognize something in me that displayed potential, which led him to give me another chance to make right in my community plagued with wrong doings.

I remember that day very clearly. He told me that there wasn't any doubt in his mind that I had committed the crimes for which I was in custody. He stated that he had sent many people to prison, so this day didn't have to be any different. Judge Goodman shared that he saw potential in me and if I was tired of going to jail I needed to get serious and begin using my influence for the greater good. He gave me a chance to make a difference and I decided to take that opportunity. After my release from jail, I began to move forward through life driven by purpose and laser focused on success.

Almost 20 years later, my new focus created space for me to become a high-ranking manager for the same probation department where I had previously spent a significant time in custody. I supervised some of the same staff members that

9

once locked me into cells. I now have a beautiful wife and five children with a wide network of family, friends and business associates and am self-employed, teaching emotional intelligence to individuals and businesses large and small across the country. It was Judge Goodman's ability to manage his emotions about the situation that cracked the door open for me to evolve and paved the way for my impact on many lives since that day.

My life experiences have prepared me to deliver the content of this book with the intent of helping someone achieve a higher level of success both personally and professionally. Simply put, if I can use what I'm about to share with you to survive the streets, beat the odds, overcome the criminal justice system and become successful in most areas of my life, then it is quite possible for *anyone* to benefit from these strategies.

The ability to 'never worry' using emotional intelligence is a unique strategy that, when infused into your daily existence, will most certainly enhance your ability to manage all the relationships connected to your life. I don't think that anyone would argue that worry and stress is counterproductive to good mental and physical health. Stress can cause illness and prevent you from enjoying life in its full capacity. Its counterpart – worry - will create a mental blockage that prohibits creativity and production. Maintaining a positive mindset takes practice and focus. Those that remain stress free are usually more at peace, happier, and can really appreciate every moment that life has to offer.

iNeverWorry is a blended mix of emotional intelligence, temperament theory, and my personal life experiences all packaged nicely for you to apply towards your personal and professional goals. These strategies can be used individually or collectively depending on what's going on around you at any given moment. The ultimate reward is having the ability to manage your emotions in a way that keeps you at peace regardless of the circumstance.

When you take a moment to really embrace these techniques, your life will be worry free and you will possess a hidden gem that most people around you don't even know exists. Every single day we cycle through a wave of emotions that impacts our decision making and interactions. Your success in life is relatively based on how you feel about yourself and others.

Most of our daily challenges stem from the lack of understanding our emotions and knowing how to manage them in the moment. Most importantly, being able to skillfully respond to the emotions of others is the most powerful tool anyone can possess. We know that education alone doesn't necessarily make you successful or the best person for the job. There are a lot of individuals that hold degrees but don't do a very good job of managing their positions. We also know people without a formal education that are highly successful and represent some of the richest companies in the world. This is not to downplay the importance of education or throw shade on anyone in particular but there is truth behind what is being said here. The way to advance and separate yourself from most people in your network is to study the fundamentals of emotional intelligence; most of us simply don't understand the power behind it or embrace it as a different kind of smart.

I didn't make up these strategies; some are extracted from the works of David Keirsey, author and creator of the Keirsey Temperament Sorter and Dr. Daniel Goleman, Ph.D., author of *Emotional Intelligence*. My goal is to share what I have learned through many years of working as a professional in the criminal justice system and present it through the lens of my personal life experiences.

I don't expect every strategy to be useful to everyone, but my hope is that you find this book a good read that is straight to the point and that you will embrace it as a valuable body of work that will remain in your reference library for many years to come.

Honorable Judge Larry Goodman   District Attorney Eileen McAndrew

2

MIND YOUR BUSINESS

Being honest with ourselves is probably the one thing we lie about the most.

Self-awareness is the ability to recognize oneself as an individual separate from the environment and other individuals. It's the ability to be completely honest with who you are in life and accepting the good with the bad. It means being very intentional about giving yourself daily reality checks in order to accurately assess who you are on a regular basis.

Everybody knows what emotions are but very few actually pay attention to them. For instance, most people will never admit their true emotional state when asked the question "What's wrong with you?" Most people will say nothing is the matter or will downplay how they actually feel. Now the only reason someone would ask that question is clearly because the energy around the other person is indicating something is going on. It seems that we are very protective of our feelings and get very uncomfortable discussing these emotions unless we are very happy or extremely angry.

If we are happy, sharing our excitement and joy is easy.

When we are mad or frustrated, complaining or criticism seems like the natural path to take. This does not apply to everyone of course, but if you begin to pay attention to those around you I guarantee you will discover that this is a true statement. Since emotions play a big part in almost every decision we make daily, it only makes sense that we give this area in our lives some attention.

The saying "I guess you woke up on the wrong side of the bed this morning" usually relates to the attitude of someone that is being unpleasant or doesn't appear to be in a good mood. Every day creates a new opportunity to bring positive energy to all those you come in contact with; however, this will be very difficult to accomplish if you don't quite understand, or aren't completely honest about the way you feel. Our moods change constantly and suddenly throughout the day. Your mood reflects the energy that radiates off of you which affects the relationships around you both personally and professionally. Imagine waking up in a great mood in the morning, because you love your job, money is flowing, health is on point and kids are on the right path. More than likely you will navigate through the day in a very positive state and if you encounter any negativity by chance it will likely not affect your day because you simply feel great.

Your personality type also plays a role in how well you respond to situations or conflicts as they arise. Now let's say things are not going so great in your life - bills aren't paid, there is conflict with friends, and you're at a job that is unfulfilling. Your outlook on life will be very different because you may angry, depressed, or frustrated. This would put you in a space to allow negative energy to give birth into your day because you are unprepared to respond appropriately due to emotional hijacking from the negative events going on around you. It's important to remember that whether you're going through good times or bad times, these are the only times we have, so let's make the best of them.

It's also quite possible you can start off the day in a good mood and in a matter of seconds some jerk cuts in front of you on the freeway. Maybe you leave home without your phone and have to turn all the way around to go get it. There is no way to control or stop things from happening to you or around you. However, there *is* a way to prepare and respond when events occur.

Let me start by being straight forward about the type of person I really am, which has always been challenging. Like most people, I find it very easy to point out the faults and challenges of others but when it comes to me, well, that's another story. I am great at giving advice but when it comes to receiving it I don't always do so well. The good part is that I am conscious of this and do my best to work on it when the moments present themselves. My mom told me the other day that I am really good at the things I like to do and not so good at the things that I don't like to do. She gave me something very real to think about. If this wasn't a true reflection of me I don't know what is. The point is that no matter what my skill level is, when I don't feel good about something then it won't get my best effort.

You see, that's what emotional intelligence is all about: knowing exactly how you feel at all times. So, before I take on any new projects or commitments in life, the first thing I must do is be completely honest about the way I feel about it and let that guide my decision.

Every morning across this country, we wake up and start our daily routine. At some point we find ourselves in front of a mirror and if you think about this for a minute, the only thing we are focused on is our outside appearance. We wash our face and brush our teeth but most of us never take the time to really look into our own eyes. It's human nature to look at others before we look at ourselves; therefore, it becomes quite easy not to mind your own business.

The next time you are standing at the mirror take an extra few moments and really look at yourself. Consider for a moment how your family and friends perceive you. Most people will say that they don't care what others think about them. However, you really should listen to what others say; there may be a tad bit of truth to what is being said. I am not saying to lose any sleep over it, but why not use the information for your own benefit and make some adjustments to better manage the relationships around you? When I say, "mind your business", I am not referring to staying out of other people's affairs. I'm speaking more to simply studying your own affairs with a focus on your emotions.

I read a statement on Facebook that credits Dave Chappelle for saying, "Our culture has accepted two huge lies. The first is that if you disagree with someone's lifestyle, you must fear or hate them. The second is that to love someone means you agree with everything they say or do. Both are nonsense, you don't have to compromise convictions to be compassionate."

Listening to the opinion of others is challenging simply because most of the time we don't like to hear feedback about ourselves unless we are being honored or praised. Seriously, just think about the feeling you get when someone critiques something about you. It doesn't matter if it's at work, play or in casual conversation. When somebody starts to describe what they see in you, most if not all of us will quickly become defensive or dismissive even if it's the absolute truth. Imagine having the ability to fully understand your temperament type and being able to embrace the behaviors that guide you towards success or failure. This can become genuinely possible if you really step outside yourself and be honest about who you really are. If I hadn't taken a step back in that courtroom, I wouldn't be where I am today. It's very difficult to see the whole picture when you are sitting inside the frame.

Maintaining a stress-free mindset is an ongoing process that requires us to consistently evaluate ourselves so that we can manage our emotions and not be offended by the circumstances that surround us. To understand emotions that run through your mind, body, and spirit you must know yourself well enough to recognize when they are occurring. Take a moment to think about how many emotions you are subject to experience at any given time. I have to constantly monitor my mood swings throughout the day. When I'm caught off guard by negative energy, it takes me a few minutes to process what just happened and calculate a positive emotional response. Most of the time, I can quickly recognize bad energy when it's in front of me and I am able to make the necessary emotional adjustments in the moment.

In my opinion there are only four basic emotions - happy, sad, fear and anger. Everything else seems to be a by-product and highlights a core emotion. We usually don't take the time to identify our emotions or own the fact that they exist. Even when we do, sometimes we don't allow ourselves time to process what's happening before we react to some external source. Having the ability to consistently remain self-aware is the cornerstone to becoming emotionally intelligent. It requires a level of honesty that is very challenging for most of us, including myself.

I work in a juvenile detention facility managing state and federal regulations, while holding personnel accountable and compliant with departmental polices. Every day I am challenged in one way or another by those who are not interested in following the rules because in this profession people have been working for so many years that they get set in doing things in their own way. This certainly isn't a reflection of everyone I work with but speaking more to the nature of the business. The point is that I must remain self-aware at all times to avoid unnecessary conflict or inappropriate responses to staff that may be disgruntled. Some of the youth that we serve struggle with conducting themselves in a respectable manner at times which means a basic conversation could lead to you be cursed out, threatened, spit at or end up in a full blown physical confrontation that ends in restraint in the blink of an eye.

Anyone who holds any position of authority knows how difficult it can be to manage multiple personalities. Whenever there is a rule change or it's time to do something different, quite often the person who is opposed to the idea will start their response with, "I just feel like...." and once that happens, we end up talking more about them than the actual issue at hand. This is true with family and friends as well. Whenever there is a disagreement, everybody wants to be heard but nobody wants to listen. As a father and a husband, I must maintain a high sense of awareness because emotions fly all over the place in family settings. Lack of emotional intelligence will have you saying things that you don't mean in the moment that you will probably regret later.

Whenever you find yourself partaking in a difficult conversation, get ahead of the game and start thinking about the best response and which feelings are associated with it. If you can put some space in between your responses then it should become pretty clear on how you can neutralize the conversation. The only way to genuinely understand your emotions is to spend enough time thinking about them to figure out where they come from and why they are there. Every time you are feeling some kind of way it definitely serves a purpose.

It is a known fact that two people can be looking at the exact same thing and see something totally different. The key is accepting that the way we perceive things becomes our reality. Just because you are not on the same page with someone doesn't always make them wrong. Whenever anyone is standing on the opposite side of any issue we automatically become opponents and we all know that the goal of a challenge is to win. Being honest about how you're feeling before you respond and embracing the perspective of others will increase the chances of arriving at a resolution.

A good way to achieve the art of minding your business is to quiet the mind. Turn off the electronic leashes we call cellphones and TV's so you can sit quietly, or simply take a peaceful walk. During these times consider some of the things that really rub you the wrong way. Replay some past scenarios in your head and see if there was anything you would do differently now that the moment has passed.

Take a look at the sentence below and ask yourself how many times you see the letter "f":

Finished files are the result of many years of scientific study combined with experience of several years.

If you show this phrase to a group of people you will get a variety of answers, ranging from 1 to 6 and the truth of the matter is that each person would be technically right. Perception is reality and the more we understand that everyone has their own perception and perspective in life, the less agitated we can become when someone doesn't agree with us. Intentionally staying focused throughout the day on how every conversation or chain of events makes you feel and literally identifying the emotion associated with them is the first step to practicing the model of "iNeverWorry."

There are a total of six occurrences of the letter "f" in the exercise above - most people forget the word "of" includes an "f". The human brain tends to see them as a "v" instead of an "f" because of our pronunciation. As you move forward, truly embrace your new perspective of intentionally remaining self-aware. Start by learning to get comfortable with being uncomfortable. This is a space that most of us run from but if you marinate in it and get familiar with the strategy, you will start to realize that you are always at an advantage as you cruise throughout your day. When you stay flexible, nobody can get you bent out of shape.

Keep in mind that there is no finish line. This is not about completion; the goal is to keep your internal software updated on the latest version of yourself.

3

MANAGING YOUR REACTIONS

Control your emotions and you will control the conversation.

It's one thing to get emotional about something and a whole different ball game when those feelings get out of control. One of the biggest human challenges is to refrain from expressing how you feel to someone in the moment. We get very intent on making sure the other person or group of people gets a piece of our mind when we get bothered or angry about a particular issue.

As we travel through these pages, I want to be clear that the intention is not to say how you should feel about stuff when it comes your way. It's really more about not letting external sources stimulate you in a way that makes you respond without giving it some thought. Being self-aware is knowing how you feel at any giving moment and actually verbalizing it to yourself so that your spirit understands what's happening. The self-control piece is deciding how you are going to channel that energy so that it doesn't cause damage to any relationship, personal or otherwise.

Inner peace really kicks in the moment you stop allowing a person or event to control your emotions. The funny thing is that we will make every excuse on why we had to get it off our chest, but the truth of the matter is that you don't. You will never have peace of mind by giving people a piece of your mind. Now, controlling your emotions is not always about negative energy. It also has to do with getting really excited about something as well. Have you ever met someone who just couldn't keep a secret? What they heard has brought them so much joy that they just had to tell somebody. This can backfire when you share some good news before the entire plan or process comes into fruition and the person you shared it with ends up sabotaging the outcome.

It might be safe to say that the negative interactions are more useful to focus on because when they are not handled properly, we usually say or do things that we can't pull back in. There is an old wise adage that says letting the cat out of the bag is much easier than getting it back in. My wife likes to say, "You can't unscramble eggs."

Take a moment to visualize what it looks like actually having a cat inside a bag, then imagine it jumping out and running around the room. Put this in perspective and you will easily understand how important it is to regulate your words before they come out. Similarly, once you drop an egg in the skillet and it starts to cook you won't be able to unscramble it; the point is most of the time when something

24

is said, it's said and you can't take it back.

I can honestly say that I have been more conscious about how I have been responding to situations ever since I was involved in a particular incident back in my early twenties. The situation has been resolved so I am OK with sharing it, but I present it only to show how one bad decision can be a game changer. At the same time in the end, like my favorite artist Tupac would say "After the darkest night always comes a brighter day."

Earlier I mentioned that growing up in Oakland came with a troublesome past. As a young adult I was making some pretty decent money which gave me the opportunity to purchase my first home at the age of twenty-three. During this time in my life things were moving really fast - I would stay up late at night and get up super early in the morning. In between those times, I would be hustling to feed my family and all those that were connected to me.

Selling drugs in your community has an interesting effect on people because when you have more money than the average resident, you become known as what we like to call a "Baller" or a "Shot Caller." During those times, I was popular because I hung on the Flatland in Brookfield which was a spot known for getting the most money and had the most respected dudes from the neighborhood.

Back then I owned a few businesses: a smoke shop, a clothing store, and a carpet cleaning service so it was very hard for me not to embrace the power that came with the hustle. The people you sell drugs to are also members of the same and neighboring community but just because they used drugs didn't necessarily mean that they didn't have families, careers or businesses themselves. This particular incident is a perfect example of how not managing your emotions no matter how much you justify it in your head can cause you to make mistakes that you may or may not be able to recover from.

This gentleman that had been buying dope from me for years also owned a roofing company. My house needed a roof and, like in hoods around the country, when we need something done we always look for the "hook up", meaning we strive to find a way to get services and goods cheaper. A new roof at the time was about $8,000 and this guy agreed to complete the job for a little less than $3,000. Because money was plentiful I gave him all of the funds up front so I could just get that issue out of the way. Like I mentioned before my daily schedule was all over the place so several weeks went by before I even realized that the work had not been completed.

When we would cross paths, he would give me excuses on why it wasn't done. I would warn him that my patience was running short and my expectation was that the task should be completed. In my mind I really thought that because I gave him a few passes, and was cool enough to let the issue slide for so long, it was justification for what happened next. Several more weeks went by and while cruising late into the night, guess who I saw walking into the corner store? Yup, you guessed it... that guy. I became so angry that I recklessly pulled my car to the curb and without taking the time to identify my emotions or make any effort to regulate them, the fight began. This brawl entailed broken beer bottles, knocked over store racks and ended in gunfire. I'm sure you can come to your own conclusion which end of the barrel I may have been on; it's the one that had me in front of the Honorable Judge Larry Goodman.

As a result, I spent the next several months away from my family, lost tens of thousands of dollars, and my businesses eventually had to be shut down. At the end of the day, what did I really accomplish? The whole situation was driven by me; I knew who I was dealing with in the first place. The minute I realized that he wasn't going to finish the work, I could have simply hired someone else to close out the job. It wouldn't have cost me much more and still would have been cheaper than the going rate at the time. No doubt it was less expensive than the money spent on lawyers and trying to pay monthly bills from a jail cell.

When he walked into the store I could have made the simple decision to keep driving. Just thinking about it today all I can do is shake my head. But the truth is that in the moment, and really all it takes is a moment, you can lose your cool and make a decision that could really impact your life.

I don't anticipate that many of my readers have gone to that extreme, but I bet there is a wide range of stories out there that by mere principle and simply based on how you feel, choices were made that became counterproductive to resolving the issue. Managing your emotions is not about dismissing how you feel; it actually has more to do with giving your emotions an identity, literally acknowledging to your spirit that you recognize their existence. Then you need to come up with your customized strategy that works for you to manage your responses, and it doesn't matter if it's a good one or a bad one. Since I have grown into a more skillful space, what works best for me is to simply be quiet and let my emotions settle. When I get overwhelmed with any type of feeling, I fall back into a Zen like space and have an internal conversation with myself.

In my head I am asking myself what feeling is associated with this event and what do I want to do about it. This works about 98% of the time. The other 2%...well, I'm still learning.

A good strategy to practice is to always remember that everything is a passing moment and that everything changes. Nothing stays the same. You have survived everything that you have ever been through, so the truth is that you will be fine when everything is all said and done.

Most importantly, take some time every single day to delete mental garbage out of your mind. Be a little selfish at some point in a 24-hour period and release all things that ɔut you heavy in thought. Take into consideration what ˌappens to your phone, computer or tablet when there are ˌoo many videos, pictures or information on them. They start ˌo operate slower and sometimes malfunction; the same ˌhing can and will happen to us if we are not careful and ˌon't pay attention.

A very simple practice you can use from now on before you respond to anything, put some space in between your responses. This will give you time to think about the most appropriate thing to say next; it doesn't have to just be when ˌhe conversation is negative. It really should be a conscious ˌhought all the time. Minding your business and consciously ˌnanaging your emotions are two great ways to be prepared ˌo skillfully respond to the feelings of others when they ɔecome problematic.

4

USING YOUR SPIDEY SENSES

The reason we have two ears and one mouth is so that we can listen twice as much as we talk. - Epictetus

This area has a lot to do with what I like to call using your Spidey Senses, or your intuition. It speaks to having the ability to pick up on all the energy in any room you enter or any person you may encounter. It's that tingling feeling inside your stomach when something just doesn't seem right. This strategy really strengthens your emotional intelligence skill set because you get a jump on how other people might be feeling and prepares you for any negative energy that might come your way.

Starting today make every encounter adventurous by scanning your surroundings and pay close attention to the body language and moods of others. Not only will this help better prepare you for upcoming conversations before they take place but also can avoid dangerous situations.

Most people don't pay attention to the body language of others as much they should. If you don't think so, just watch how the majority of folks are busy on their phones, deep in conversation or just simply being impersonal the next time you are out in public. You can gather some pretty good information by simply observing the actions of others.

Check out their facial expressions and postures; see who is engaging in conversation and who is standoffish. Once you have taken the time to really observe the energy in the room, then you can start calculating how you want your interactions to take place. This will not take away any of your time but instead will put you in a state of social awareness.

There is a reason sports teams go back and look at tapes after games. They want to go frame by frame to check out player's moves and strategies so that they can prepare for the next game. Since we don't have the luxury of going back and looking at video footage of our lives and interactions, we have to practice the same technique before the conversation game even starts.

When people are in a bad mood it is usually not hard to recognize, but if you are not paying attention you might ask them questions or engage in conversation that is counterproductive because of the energy. Of course, this type of behavior is never really excusable but by recognizing others' moods you could possibly avoid unnecessary conflict. Opportunities are often missed at work or in business by simply talking to someone about the wrong thing at the wrong time. Being in alignment with the energy of the universe is something that can be of great benefit if you take the time to tune in to it. We all have it inside of us, you just have to tap into it. Think about all the times you should have followed your first mind - that time right before you hit something or something hits you. Maybe something happened at a place that you had just left or you entered a relationship that you knew from the beginning was all bad. Or when you are in a bad space in your life but something inside of you tells you that everything is going to be all right and you believe it.

All of these are examples of those intuitive Spidey Senses and they should not be reserved exclusively for use in extreme cases. Rather, remain conscious of them all the time. I'm always tuned in for the most part, so much so that I don't even think about how my day is going to start or end. When I wake up in the morning there is nothing about me that plans on how to face the day, my attitude is to *embrace* the day. I'm going to let my spirit guide me in whichever direction I am supposed to go in. It can be as simple as which direction I drive to work or what I'm going to eat for the day.

I remember a time when my managers and I were in Pennsylvania for training and we were walking down the street looking for a bite to eat. They kept asking me where we were going to eat and I kept saying, "I don't know! Wherever the energy takes us!" There were so many restaurants to choose from and they were all very crowded. Then instantly something told me to cross the street and boom! I stumbled upon this nice Mexican restaurant that had some of the best authentic food I've ever tasted. There was no waiting time and they had a private patio where we sat and people watched while enjoying a nicely priced quality meal. I point this out to say it doesn't have to be an over-the-top thought process. It's the little things that keep you in practice for when the bigger situations happen.

My decision to get remarried after a 12-year relationship with my ex-wife is more proof that following your intuition can be of great benefit. Like most divorces, mine was pretty ugly and very emotional. I stayed depressed, frustrated and ashamed for a long period of time. Nothing about that separation worked in my favor, I mean absolutely nothing. I walked away from community property, I could see my youngest son only twice a week, I gave up half my retirement and so much more. I share this to say that emotionally I wasn't in any space to be open to another relationship. In fact, I actually planned to remain single for the rest of my life, feeling like there wasn't any actual benefit to ever getting married again.

It would have been easy to ignore the growing bond that Casie and I were beginning to build for obvious reasons. As we began hanging out with each other more and more, our conversations started leaning towards a relationship. I was so apprehensive and protective of my heart that I had serious reservations. The point in all of this is that if I didn't take time to marinate in my feelings and be honest with myself about how they were affecting my outlook on life, I could have missed this remarkable opportunity to have a companion that is as compassionate and supportive as Mrs. Bedford. Even though I had built walls around my heart, my Spidey Senses kept tingling, signaling that this was a good thing. Truth be told, she helped me position myself physically and mentally to even get these words on paper. Despite all my past behaviors and things I struggle with in the present, she stays true to who she is and intuitively sees the bigger picture. She also had to embrace the skills of managing her emotions to cope with all the challenges that come with blending families and coping with baggage that comes from previous relationships.

Now let me change lanes a bit and share another interesting story about a time when being emotionally intelligent was very challenging. However, by following these strategies there was an interesting outcome.

Once my criminal record from back in the day was expunged I had the opportunity to apply for a job at the Alameda County Probation Department. I was so excited to have a fresh start and put all my energy into doing whatever it took to qualify for the position. I was putting in countless volunteer hours working back in the courtroom, helping those that were coming up behind me so they didn't have to go through all the struggles I did.

In 1999, I was given the National Spirit of Youth Award from the Coalition of Juvenile Justice which was the first of its kind; I was the very first recipient of this award. There is a lot of newspaper and media articles that can be found by

Googling my name showing the amount of work that was being accomplished. They wouldn't hire me because of my background, even though everything had been cleared. This was very discouraging to say the least, but I was determined and resilient. If you know anything about the Civil Service Exam process you know that it can take upwards of nine months to get through the testing process. I went through it twice and ranked in the top five percent each time.... only to be denied via an impersonal letter that didn't give any insight on what I could have done better in order to get hired. By now, I was ready to give up but my emotions were in check and I decided to apply again after the one year waiting period required after each denial.

Here is where it gets deep: while going through the testing process again I was out in my old neighborhood one day and stumbled across a group of young men shooting dice on the corner. They were known as the Nut Case Killers, (more info about this group can be found on Google). What made me stop and talk with them was because they had been stealing cars from the local rental car company and driving recklessly all over the neighborhood, making it unsafe for the elderly and young children. Since this was my old stomping grounds, and these guys were only babies when I was hustling back in the day, I thought that this conversation would be respectable and easy. My intention was to encourage them to stop driving so recklessly or at least take it outside the community. Man, was I wrong; one of the guys who I literally watched grow up became confrontational and wasn't being reasonable at all.

He instantly rallied his comrades and jumped into a car and sped off. The remainder of the fellas and I continued to talk because they understood where I was coming from. Next thing I know, several gunshots were being fired at me as they sped back around the corner. Now, growing up in Oakland, the one thing that we all pretty much agree on is that if somebody pulls a gun out, and especially if they use it, it means war...period point blank.

This is where this all becomes relevant: even though I had the full capability to retaliate and certainly wasn't a stranger to gun play, I was at enough peace with myself not to respond. I was extremely angry and there was a lot of pressure from my peers to not let this incident just pass. But again, by this time I was learning how to mind my business, manage my emotions, and my Spidey Senses were indicating that this would not end well if I wasn't careful. So I followed my intuition and let the incident go. About six months later, I was hired at the Alameda County Probation Department. Several months later all those guys were on the local news and had been arrested for multiple murders and robberies. The irony was that one of the main players ended up in custody in the same unit I was working in at Juvenile Hall. Instead of holding a grudge, I decided to help him during this difficult time in his life since he was only 16 years old and facing upwards of 25 years to life. I believe all of them ended up with about 75 years collectively in prison.

If I hadn't paid attention to those Spidey Senses, I may have been the one with all that prison time. Fourteen years later, I am at the peak of my career and unfortunately, they are walking the prison yards. Again, you may never encounter a crisis like this in your lifetime but if I can find the space inside of me to manage my emotions when, in my mind I had every reason not to, then surely you can in less intense situations. Like I stated before, opportunities can be missed when you're too involved in your feelings and don't know what to do with them.

5

MANAGING RELATIONSHIPS

The toughest job you may ever hold is managing all the different relationships that have an impact on your life.

The one thing that is truly missing in every relationship is taking the time to identify the nature of the relationship and establishing how to behave when conflict arises. Establishing the nature of the relationship can be a little uncomfortable because it requires asking questions like "Are we friends?" "Are we just coworkers?" "Are we dating?" "Is this just business?" This may seem a little corny but think about how many times in your life that it wasn't until later down the road, the type of relationship you thought you had with someone was not what you expected it to be. This goes for friends, couples, business associates and everything in between.

The other piece to this is being upfront with the things that can rub you the wrong way and how you behave when that happens. By having this type of discussion, the framework of expectations is set, and it gives everyone a heads up on how to move faster towards a solution instead of amplifying the problem.

When it comes to managing relationships with the people around you, the best way to gauge their moods is by noticing their body language and the look in their eyes. Body language refers to the nonverbal signals that we use to communicate. According to some experts, these nonverbal signals make up a huge part of daily communication. From our facial expressions to our body movements, the things we *don't* say can still convey volumes of information. In many cases, you should look at signals as a group rather than focusing on a single action. One thing that can be a challenge is listening without anticipating jumping in the conversation, much like teenage girls trying to play a game of Double Dutch. It's important to let the communication flow naturally and be OK with allowing the person you're talking to have control of the conversation, if necessary.

Think about the feeling that starts to develop if you are struggling to get your point across in a conversation with someone. Most of the time it won't happen if they are dead set on leading, so why bother? Whatever information you have still has value and really, the other person just missed out. Let's be honest. Most people who are absorbed in their own feelings have difficulty relaying their thoughts through conversation and can cause some tension. I know some folks that can hold a grudge or a bad attitude for days, weeks or even months.

Depending on the scenario, relationships can be damaged

over something really small. What makes all of this important is that by recognizing early warning signs and body language, you can judge whether it's the right moment to engage. Also, by regulating your own feelings and giving yourself some space to respond will increase the chances of ending with good results. You will always put yourself at an advantage regardless of the nature of the relationship.

I continue to work on this skill set because there have been times that I have failed to read the emotional field with family and friends. I would just be engaged in the conversation, not aware that they were burning up inside. I didn't pick up on the mood in the moment. The more I continued to talk, the more agitated they became. Most of the time they would not share with me that they were mad, but instead held some level of resentment. The next time we talked, I couldn't figure out how our simple issues became so complicated to discuss. Now I know it was because I missed the signals and disregarded their feelings. This can easily occur with your spouse, children and friends. Not only should you pay attention to the energy of others, but most importantly the mood or demeanor *you* bring into the room.

For example, I have been told that when I walk into a room, I come off as authoritative; some people actually mistake me for being cocky at times. Honestly, I don't see myself that way, but since some people do, I've started to become more conscious of it. Even though I might just be in heavy thought, or I'm just walking with confidence, my body language can create negative energy without any intention at all. This certainly could affect different relationships around me.

When most people reference the word "relationship" they are usually talking about two individuals that represent a couple. If you are in a relationship with someone right now then you know it takes time and attention to develop and maintain that relationship if you want to keep it in good standing. Many relationships fail as soon as we stop nurturing them. In life, anything that you don't water will die; positive energy should be your responsibility in every relationship you are involved in. The part that most of us don't understand is that every relationship around you is of importance and deserves attention. In business or at work, this is more critical than you think simply because we never know who knows who and what influence they may have on something you may need down the road.

Many people tend to be vocal about their dislike for someone, which is not a smart move in my opinion. Once the rumors get started, it can be very hard to control the damage afterwards. In my line of work, some of the staff I supervise often complain about the decisions that come from my office. Over time the conversation moves in the direction of how they personally don't like the things that I am doing, but they never come and have a direct conversation with me which I always find to be very interesting. Before you know, my name is in the rumor mill and people are talking about me and the situation without having any facts. Naturally, this bothers me at times because it's really unnecessary and I can't wrap my head around why it's so natural to tear each other down instead of working to build each other up. This is where the iNeverWorry model comes into play. I certainly don't like gossip and every now and then I want to confront them and get down to the core of the problem. However, since I now exercise a different kind of smart, I am able to identify and channel my feelings appropriately. I can confidently engage in conversation with people who have been slandering my name and they have no clue that I am fully aware of their motives. This keeps me at an advantage at all times because they have exposed their hand, while mine is still tucked away. My future moves are calculated like a chess move and theirs are jumping all over the place, like a game of checkers. I make the necessary adjustments and I am always at peace, while they are busy worrying about me. This same strategy is applicable with so-called friends, especially with some of the ones on Facebook.

I never block or delete someone on social media for being disloyal, or those who gossip. These folks are perfect for free promotion and it just burns them up when they see you constantly growing and doing well. They wonder why you are not bothered by the negativity. I know exactly what my emotional state is and know how to compartmentalize my feelings without them ever knowing where I stand.

When it comes to family or friends, it's not any different; why waste time breathing life into anything less than positive? Always give yourself space to think about what is happening in front of you, and take pride in being the most emotionally intelligent person in the room. The moment you master this concept, you will without a doubt be at more peace and focused than the person you are engaging in conversation with.

The other side of this is how you manage the positive relationships in your life. I know this might sound a little awkward, but I think most of us are guilty of mismanaging our relationships. In this age of technology, we have become so connected to smart phones and tablets that we are disconnected from each other. Think about what happens on your birthday or special holidays - we get hundreds of texts and very little, if any, actual phone calls. It has gotten so bad that when we do talk on the phone with someone, it seems like a special conversation.

No wonder why some of us struggle with basic conversations; we are out of practice with live communication. I see it when we have applicants come in for job interviews. We know they have the credentials on paper, but when it comes to articulating their message the struggle is real. To increase your chances for success at a job interview, it's important to have your emotions together, calculate your responses, and maneuver around the energy of the interviewers. The next conversation you engage in, try to intentionally watch body language and try to tune into what kind of energy is being generated. Just paying attention to this alone will help the conversation manifest into a positive one, or at the least make the already good conversation much smoother.

In the criminal justice field, I have noticed some of our staff have great relationships with clients, and others are problematic. The difference between the two is the ability to communicate effectively and manage the relationships. Another way to strengthen relationships is to make an effort to remember people's names when you meet them and periodically use it during the conversation when appropriate.

Solid relationships are something that should be sought after. They are the result of how you understand people, how you the treat them, and the history you share. The weaker the connection you have with someone, the harder it will be to get your point across. Think about all the people with whom you have great relationships. Those conversations are always the easiest, and the people with whom we have less than desirable connections are the ones that are most difficult to get your point across.

One way to move through challenging discussions is to acknowledge the feelings or message that is coming from the other person. We have to get comfortable with giving up some small wins in order to get to the bigger victory, which is communicating effectively. If you are stressed out, this will always interfere with your ability to communicate at your best. The only way to cope with stress is by accepting and understanding the circumstance that created it in the first place. Stress is usually caused when your expectations don't match reality. In other words, whatever it is that you really want to happen is not happening, and that causes frustration, which then leads to stress. I mentioned before that people are your greatest resource and this is something that I hold in high regard, even in my worst relationships. I try to work on those types of relationships, but only at the right time and the appropriate moments. If you have children you know that these can be some of the most challenging relationships to maintain. One of the best ways to improve conversations with them is to make sure you let them have a voice. As adults, we are quick to tell our kids what we think is best for them, or we want them to know how we used to do things back when we were growing up. One day I was talking with my daughter Jazmyne about cleaning her bathroom, and during the discussion I hit her with the ol' "You don't know how it used to be when I was growing up. We had to share a bathroom with the whole house as well as the same bedroom" speech. She looked at me and said, "Daddy, you're right. I don't understand. I have always had my own bathroom and bedroom so I wouldn't know the difference." Ever since that conversation, I do my best to look at things from their perspective to become more knowledgeable on how they may be feeling. The lesson for me was clear: if you want to be understood in life then first you must learn to understand.

6

TEMPERAMENT THEORY

Exercising Emotional Intelligence is what keeps you mentally strong.

Temperament Theory is something I discovered in a training class back in 2009. If you have worked at one of those jobs that requires tons of training then you most definitely understand me when I say that I'm never excited about sitting in class for eight hours with a monotone instructor.

The subject matter presented was about a new federal government initiative, which really supported my belief that this training was about to be extremely boring. However, I was intrigued when they started talking about a methodology for helping people understand human behavior. I discovered that people naturally think and talk about what they are interested in, and when you listen carefully to people's conversations, you find two broad but distinct areas of subject matter. Each of us is born with a temperament, which is our natural way of understanding, communicating, and interacting with the world. Some people talk primarily about the external concrete world of everyday reality. Other people talk primarily about the internal abstract world of ideas. At times, of course, everyone addresses both sorts of topics in their daily lives At every turn people are trying to accomplish their goals, and if you watch closely how people go about their business, you see that there are two fundamentally opposite types of action.

Some people are focused on getting results, achieving their objectives as effectively or efficiently as possible, and only afterwards do they check to see if they are observing the rules or going through proper channels. Other people act primarily in a cooperative or socially acceptable manner. That is, they try to do the right thing, keeping with social rules and standards, conventions, and codes of conduct, and only later do they concern themselves with the effectiveness of their actions.

These two ways of acting can overlap, but people instinctively will do what works, while others do what's right. There is plenty of research out there to support temperament theory and its several different approaches. The challenge is trying to find the method that is easy to understand and one that works well for you. I will do my best to simplify the various temperaments, then you can decide which temperament you are most likely to possess.

Going back to the outcome of the training, I decided to become a certified facilitator of Temperament Theory because the model was very simple and easy to understand. There are basically four different temperament styles; depending on where you learn it the instructor may use colors, numbers or animals to describe each component. For the sake of this reading, I will break them down by the names I created.

iNeverWorry is a model that is designed to better manage your emotions and to strategically respond to the emotions of others. By fully understanding all of the components, I will step out on a limb and say that your communication will improve and you will have healthier relationships all around you.

We all have our unique temperament type and when communicating with each other it can be problematic when we don't understand where the other person is coming from. The more we learn about communication styles and begin to accept each other's temperaments without judgment then we create space for relationships to strengthen.

Truly accepting someone for who they are means you accept their actions, ideas, and communication techniques. One thing I need to point out is that we all have some of the four temperament traits in us, more than likely one of these will most closely represent how you operate most of the time.

The best way to explain it is for you to do this exercise: grab a pen/pencil and write your name down three times.

Now after you have done that, I want you to write it again but this time use your opposite hand. I know, I know. Just try it. Once you have completed this task, think for a moment how easy it was to write your name with the hand you use most often. You didn't even have to think about it. When it came to the hand you never use, I'm sure you had to concentrate a little harder and it was probably sloppy, but if you stayed focused I know you did it. We all operate in our primary temperament without effort, very much like writing our name, the secondary and beyond exist in you but may require some thought in order to access the traits that come with them.

Depending on where you are in life, and what you are doing, you will naturally access the relevant temperament to match the climate. Commonly, some people recognize that they may operate in a specific temperament while at work and may slide into another one when they get home.

7

THE ORGANIZER

Never settle for being average; it's too close to the bottom and too far from the top.

The Organizer speaks mostly of their duties and responsibilities, and what they can keep an eye on and take good care of. They are careful to obey the laws, follow the rules, and respect the rights of others. You can count on them to stick to the task at hand and see it all the way through, and they are usually the person you want to go to when you need to get the job done efficiently. They are highly responsible, neat, and well organized. They are not comfortable playing around until the work gets done.

This group has a real problem when things are unorganized or not structured; they can't stand it when things are that way. For the most part, they are serious minded and have a conservative and traditional view when it comes to love. They are very hard working and hold punctuality in high regard. In their minds being early is being on time. When it comes to planning and keeping things in order, this is the group you want in your corner. For me, this temperament type is like writing with the opposite hand; I struggle with structure and prefer to multitask rather than stick to one thing at a time. Whenever I have a deadline for a report or policy revision, I am very last minute. The deadline for this book to go to the editor was submitted at the 11th hour, and my wife joked with me about getting a kick out of working under pressure. This will make more sense when we get to my temperament type.

Every training I have facilitated or trip I have taken didn't get my full attention until the day before or even the morning of the event. If just the thought of things happening last minute makes you cringe a little, then you probably fit this category. My manager represents this group so I know that when it's time to submit any reports to her they need to be on point. She is big on grammar and sentence structure. By understanding this, I know she is not being a difficult boss, it's just the way she processes information. The beauty of our working relationship is that we understand each other's temperaments, so in turn she gives me the flexibility to be creative in my assignment and doesn't put me under tight time constraints. At the same time, she makes me better because I know I have to double check my work before I submit it to her.

When I first came under her direct supervision the first thing I did was sit down with her and have a meeting. In that conversation I asked her what her pet peeves were, and what things drove her absolutely crazy. Most people would not have such a conversation with their manager, but I understand the importance of gathering information so that I can navigate accordingly. Knowing ahead of time what to look out for or to avoid only gives our working relationship space to grow. It has given us an opportunity to come together on departmental conflicts, as well as some dynamic projects over the last three years.

People that have this trait can come off a little pushy if you are not aware of how they naturally function. Their work area is usually very organized, and they would prefer that if there is a change in something that they be notified soon as possible. They usually have things well planned out and prepared. In their financial lives they do pretty well with balancing everything because they have a habit of keeping lists in an effort to maintain order. The best way to keep a conversation going smoothly with them is to cut the small talk and get straight to the point. Honesty goes a long way with them and they prefer you keep the conversation in order, and not get side tracked. Be sure to focus on whatever issue or task that needs to get done, keep them tied into their role in the discussion so that they stay interested.

By their very nature, they view things as black or white and right or wrong. To them, there is one way to do something and it is the right way - also known as "their" way. They are quick decision makers. In times of conflict, they may doggedly stand by their decision which exacerbates conflicts with a person who sees several options or multiple solutions. They endeavor to maintain control of both themselves and the situation. The thought of losing control causes fear and anxiety and in a stressful situation, they may tend to reach for closure before considering all of the options. They can become entrenched in the "one right way". They can be viewed as inflexible and resistant to change. Additionally, they do not intentionally welcome or encourage conflict, nor do they avoid it. When difficult issues arise and they are unable to maintain their usual structure, organization, planning, decisiveness, and idea of what is right, they can become overly structured and rigid and disinclined to engage in any negotiations.

Fortunately, people in this group are "fixers" and they have an innate desire to make things right. It does not serve their purpose to allow conflict to fester or to become unmanageable. Allow them time to calm down and to process their thoughts and decisions, and they will likely return with a plan for resolution. When seeking resolution with them, be sure to define the issue, be respectful, and take responsibility for your actions. This temperament style comes in handy for me when it's really time to tighten down and get things done.

8

THE PEACEFUL SPIRIT

The man I am today is carved out of the guy I was yesterday.

The Peaceful Spirits are nurturing by nature with vivid imaginations, and they love to talk with others about the way they feel. They are not a huge fan of conflict and usually will shy away from confrontation. They move through life with their heart and deeply care about others.

They are very loving, they nurture that love to encourage others, and really want to see everyone succeed. People in this group are great communicators and tend to be spiritual or earthy people that look for the true meaning or real significance of life. This temperament type is usually very family oriented and makes the best type of friend because they will always be genuinely concerned about your true well-being. They will also be strong advocates for you in your absence. They will take a firm stance for justice when it comes to the rights of the people. You have to be prepared to talk a little longer with them than other groups. It's important to them that they cover all the concerns that may arise in the conversation and they tend to repeat themselves a few times along the way.

Emotions are usually at an elevated level simply because they lead with their heart. However, don't mistake them for being soft because everything is driven by feeling - they will be very intense when something is not going so well. In times of conflict, these same traits can cause them difficulty. They are averse to conflict. In other words, they would rather avoid or ignore situations or discussions that may result in confrontation or conflict. Conflict for them is uncomfortable, unnecessary, and unpleasant. They will even go so far as make excuses for poor or inappropriate behavior so as not to generate any ill will or any type of confrontation. Sometimes they may actually blame themselves for the failings of others. All of this tends to be unhealthy for them because they also personalize everything, even things that were not meant to be personal.

Some temperaments are fairly direct and at times very blunt. Peaceful Spirits may interpret that as anger, frustration, unfriendliness or "they simply don't like me". They would rather give in before an issue is resolved to re-establish harmony. In failing to deal with an issue, they are essentially stuffing the issue into a sack that they drag around with them. After a while, the sack becomes quite heavy and burdensome and at some point, the sack will be unable to hold one more problem. When the bag explodes, the emotional outpouring can be overwhelming.

The first step in managing a relationship with a Peaceful Spirit is to recognize when they are not their usual happy selves. Of course, if you ask them if they are OK they will tell you they are fine. That is code for, "I am not fine". Pressuring them to tell you what is wrong will not work. Instead, extend the offer if they want to talk at some later date, you are willing to listen. Sincerity is paramount. This group intuitively knows when someone is saying the right words but is actually disinterested in dealing with them. When they do want to talk, your only job is to listen. Again, listen attentively; don't fake it. Be pleasant and show empathy for their concerns. Focus on the people aspects when searching for a resolution. Always allow plenty of time for them to express their feelings. It's always best to give them the opportunity to have their concerns and feelings heard and validated.

If you happen to be the offending party, taking responsibility for your part in the conflict is critical. Acknowledge what you did or said, offer a sincere apology, and do not repeat the offending behavior. The Peaceful Spirit will then be quick to forgive and move on.

This is my secondary temperament. It's the part of me that makes it easy for me to communicate well with youth and is the space I tap into when I'm consulting or training. For my wife, this is her primary, which is why we get along so well. It's funny though, before we recognized each other's temperaments, I couldn't understand why she wanted to talk so much about everything. After learning about this theory, it made perfectly good sense.

9

THE ANALYZER

Stay committed to your decisions, but flexible with your approach.

The Analyzer group represents an expression of logic and they are great researchers. They usually demonstrate a composed demeanor using mind over emotion to orchestrate and solve the mysteries of life. They are non-conforming by nature and usually think in abstract terms. This group is very independent and sometimes people may think they are impersonal. That's not the case; they are just more comfortable with things than people. Seeking knowledge is what makes them happy and they very rarely talk about their feelings.

Keep your conversations factual with this group and straight to the point. When you tell them something, don't get bothered when they probably won't believe you until they get the facts behind what is being said. They must respect someone before they value their advice; it's common for them to ponder and struggle over decisions to be certain that they don't make any mistakes. Nothing is black and white and to them possibilities are endless.

What may be conflict for others may be a vigorous debate for this group. They don't become very agitated.

However, they can be relentless in pursuing the facts, following logic to ensure that you understand. They may continue a debate until their opponent concedes, they agree to disagree, or through some odd twist of fate, they are proven wrong.

They are logical, analytical, objective, and autonomous information gatherers. These same traits can lead to turmoil in times of stress and conflict. The Analyzer can become too analytical and fail to recognize the impact of their decisions on others. They miss emotional signals and other people's needs. They can appear cold, disassociated, and unsympathetic. Sometimes they may actually see too many options and thus have trouble bringing conflict to a conclusion because there is always more data emerging leading to more potential solutions and conclusions. They also may fail to give due consideration to time pressure and priorities because they may "over think" the problem. When this group becomes displeased with a situation, they withdraw to a place of solitude where they can be alone with their thoughts. They will analyze situations, process thoughts, consider the facts, formulate a conclusion and then execute a plan. The amazing part is that this entire scenario could unfold completely unbeknownst to any other party. They have a remarkable ability to self-resolve.

This temperament is the one that I personally use the least. I don't really concern myself much with validating what people say or do. For me, I take everything at face value which often gets me the short end of a deal because I don't dig deeper for details. I am open to working with almost everybody and tend to trust people easily.

iNeverWorry

10

THE CREATIVE SPIRIT

Live your life so that you are too busy to worry by day and too sleepy to worry at night.

The Creative Spirit promotes action, motivation and excitement. This group urges you to wake up and seize the moment, make quick decisions, and take advantage of opportunities as soon as they are available. Their personality encourages a playful atmosphere of activity and movement.

They are fun-loving by nature with lots of energy to go out and try new things. They are very comfortable pursuing new adventures and don't mind being the life of the party, or showing off their talents and skills. One of the things that doesn't sit well with others is they tend to get bored easily and will get restless with structured jobs or activities.

Most entrepreneurs possess these traits because they are motivated by the notion of creating something great or being responsible for the next big thing. This temperament type are your go-getters, trend setters and risk takers. Quite often they are mistaken for not taking work or life seriously, but they are actually really hard workers who make things look easy. They require little or no direction from others; once they get the idea of what needs to get done they do it, and on their own terms.

It's not uncommon for them to frustrate others because they are very confident and can come off nonchalant about issues that may be of serious concerns to others. They generally confront issues head on and jump in immediately to solve a problem or address a challenge. Since they naturally display high energy and excitement in a situation involving conflict, they may become very expressive, using a loud voice and animated gestures. As they are speaking louder and faster, they are also listening less because they want to be sure to express their viewpoint. At times, they may lack a filter between the brain and the mouth so they might say things they regret later.

While their outbursts can be explosive, they do not hold onto anger or feelings after the outburst. Once they vent their frustrations, they move on. They are forward moving people and don't look back. This group will always see the big picture, so in a heated discussion, they are not inclined to focus on details. They may miss the obvious or "forget" inconvenient details.

Humor is one method they will use to defuse conflict. Don't mistake that for a lack of seriousness. Do be prepared for them to challenge the issue at hand. They will be direct and at times, rather blunt. Listen to their thoughts and try not to focus on how they are communicating to you. It is the message, not the delivery, that is important. Be flexible and realistic, and offer alternatives. Allow them to decide how they will accomplish the task they are given. These people need to have some freedom of movement along with the freedom to do it their way. Just letting them use their creativity and try something new is very empowering and motivating for them.

They are trailblazers, so let them do what they do best. Be sure to provide a due date. Also, leave them alone, even when it appears they are playing around and not getting the task completed. They will complete it, and they will complete it on time.

Since they get bored rather easily, they tend to start a task or project and then move on to something else before completing what they originally started. They can be working on multiple projects in various stages of completion.

These temperament types are not linear thinkers and they are not detail oriented. This is challenging for the Organizer and Analyzer. who tend to be more structured and process oriented. The Creative Spirit does not operate in this manner. They are burst workers and will likely wait until very close to the deadline before making a real concerted effort to get the job done. Their chaotic and frenetic pace mystifies other temperaments who would be stressed by the pressure of a looming deadline that is now upon them only because they waited so long to get started. They work best under pressure, and conflict arises when others try to micromanage whatever task at hand.

This is my personal primary temperament type, and I can honestly say that I love being a Creative Spirit. It has helped me overcome many challenges in my life. I stay in a constant state of development and usually am willing to make moves that a lot of people wouldn't dare to take on. Operating in my natural capacity always gives me a unique perspective on everyday occurrences and, as an example, the creativity to deliver you the content of this book (with more editions to follow!).

11

MOODS & ATTITUDES

Your attitude determines your altitude.

Often, your attitude is the number one factor that determines your level of success. By maintaining a positive attitude in life, you're almost certain to reach your goals, while at the same time building stronger relationships around you. Managing relationships with people with negative attitudes can be a very frustrating experience. However, your attitude is self-chosen, and you can control whether or not you want to be in a positive or negative mood.

It is your responsibility to change your attitude when it's not positive or as powerful as it needs to be for the day. Attitudes are not given to you, they are created by you. Most people know when they are in a bad mood, but very few can see the consequences of their own negative attitudes. Your mood is powerful and can be the determining factor that makes or breaks a business deal. There will always be events happening around us, and at times, things just seem to be happening to us. Life has a very unique way of humbling us; one day you can be sitting at the table and the next day you can be on the menu.

The way you perceive things will make all the difference in the world. Moods are contagious and can rub off on those around you. I know coworkers that seem to always be in a bad mood, no matter how beautiful the day is outside. People with negative attitudes show the least respect to others and often expect you to validate or care that they are having a bad day. Some will stay in a constant state of rudeness while others spend their time criticizing everybody and everything around them. As soon as they enter a room, the positive energy gets sucked out like someone just turned on a vacuum. Their perspective on life totally impedes on their chances of doing great things. They can hear an opportunity knocking, but will just complain about the noise and ignore the purpose behind the knock. In my profession, we have to work with clients on an individual basis as well as in groups. The quality of service we provide is directly related to the moods of our staff, which greatly impacts the chances of success with our clients. Poor attitudes create strained relationships. A ripple effect is created in the community when a client doesn't benefit from the resources that could have been available if there was good rapport within the working relationship.

I recently attended a grand opening for a local lounge. There was a pretty good vibe and everything was completely chill. I decided to make my way to the bar where there were two bartenders working. The first thing that I noticed was all the negative energy coming from the both of them.

Because their attitudes were foul, every person they served had some type of confrontational response, which slowed down the service drastically. Although I came in a good mood, my attitude started to change after witnessing these guys slam glasses down, question drink orders, and ignore customers. I quickly realized that my emotional status was sliding into frustration, so I decided that it was best to just walk away. It would have been easy to add to the confusion by expressing my dislike of having to wait for a drink that never came. However, I headed back to my table and explained to my friends why I was in front of them empty handed. This created negative energy and mood swings immediately because everyone started complaining and feeling bothered. I had been waiting at the bar for about 30 minutes, and my friends were ready to eat and drink, but were disappointed when I returned empty handed. As people passed by our table to say hello, they got an earful on how poor the service had been for the evening.

Moments later, the manager came to our table and with a calm demeanor, I briefly explained to him what my experience had been at his establishment. The manager responded by getting us the food and drinks we ordered quickly. He was kind enough to discount our bill and apologized for the inconvenience. However, since the cat was already out of the bag, there was not much damage control he could do at that point. Those two rude bartenders delivered poor service, which consequently created a loss of revenue for the owner because he had to discount product and give away free items. Even bigger than that, especially on an opening night, there inevitably would be negative reviews floating around, which may impact future business. Just think about how all those conversations about the service go viral on social media, as well as word of mouth reviews to the patron's family and friends. That's a pretty hefty price to pay for employees that lack emotional intelligence; it's just bad for business. To take it a step further, those bartenders didn't have a clue on what potential resources were available through any one of their customers. They could easily have jeopardized future opportunities if they ever crossed paths again with those customers.

Conversely, I have witnessed an awesome display of what a positive attitude looks like from one of my colleagues we called Uncle J. He came to work every single day with a bright smile on his face and intentionally brought positive energy into any space he entered. He was always in a great positive space, which made anybody's mood in his presence swing from low to high. Not one time did I ever witness him get mad at anybody during the many years we worked together. One day, Uncle J became terminally ill very unexpectedly. However, he still reported to work every single day like nothing was wrong. He was rapidly losing weight and was fatigued all the time, and you could see the disease all over his face. Uncle J was disappearing right before our eyes. No doubt, we were more emotional about his condition than him.

During this time, I was struggling financially and felt emotionally hijacked from dealing with civil legal matters. I came to work one day in a bad mood and ran into Uncle J in the hallway, and as usual he was a walking around like a motivational quote ready for a live status update. As we started talking, I saw the pain in his eyes, but Uncle J stood there with his head up and shoulders back, mentoring our youth, giving advice, and spreading love, when he could have been at home resting. During our conversation, he gave me some great words of encouragement. I walked away feeling so much better about life and realized, in that moment, that if he could remain extremely positive through a painful terminal illness, then how dare I complain about the trivial obstacles in my life that always end up becoming a passing moment anyway. Uncle J lost his battle with the disease a short time later, but his positive spirit lives on through his countless family and friends.

What is attitude anyway? It is the mental state or position you take regarding your life and affairs. Your attitude forms every event in your life, whether you realize it or not. Every day, your attitude is challenged by other people and by external factors. Will you allow a negative person to ruin your day, make you lose your cool, or force you to give up on your dreams? When the temptation to slide into a negative mindset comes knocking on your door, stand at the door of your mind and declare powerfully and silently, "No one is home". In other words, just because someone else has issues doesn't mean you have to subscribe to them.

At certain junctures in our lives, we will inevitably encounter challenging circumstances and people. We can either regard our dilemmas with anger, bitterness or frustration, or we can look deep within and find the source that is beyond all circumstances, pick ourselves up and move forward, knowing all things will work in our favor. If, on any given day, negative drama surrounds you, hang on to your own positive attitude and don't let other people drag you down. Your moods can differ from your temperament or personality traits, which are longer lasting. We can be sent into a mood by an unexpected event - the happiness of seeing an old friend or the anger of discovering betrayal by a partner. The truth of the matter is that some days we will just have mood swings and that's OK, as long as we stay tapped into our emotional intelligence skill sets and remember that everything will turn out just fine.

iNeverWorry

12

PATIENCE

Some days will teach us patience and other days will test it.

The art of being patient is one of the most important – and most difficult – aspects of maintaining emotional intelligence. You will need to practice being patient every day in order to tie all the components of iNeverWorry all together. It sounds more difficult that it is; in most cases people simply don't want to wait around for anything. Patience is the capacity to accept or tolerate delay, trouble, or suffering without getting angry or upset. Start paying close attention to how you feel whenever you have to wait for anything. This can happen at the street light, in line at the grocery store, getting gas, on the phone, in the elevator, etc. Every day, situations will test you on how well you can be patient. It takes a concentrated effort and some time before the strategies here become second nature to you. You have to practice writing with that opposite hand. To get the best results, pick one of the strategies and practice it all day long. Keep your antennas up and seek out opportunities to test the model and see how they work for you.

Modern society is very impatient. We want our food

fast, we want fast money, fast conversation, fast relationships, fast entertainment, fast education, some want fast cars, and many want fast solutions to problems in life. Few of us take time out from the rat race to really analyze and think about the life which we are living and many actually want to live in the future. If you are not learning new skills and gaining new knowledge then you will probably be stuck with your mood swings well into the unforeseeable future. Sometimes it's not until a life changing crisis happens which causes you to consciously change your lifestyle of impulsive impatience.

One of the most powerful lessons I have learned along the way is patiently waiting for things to work themselves out and let the moments pass. Think about something you went through in the last year that may have had you bummed out. Today that situation probably doesn't even matter to you. Even if the situation still holds some space in your life, more than likely it's not as intense as it was at the time it occurred. The truth is, time heals all wounds unless you pick at them. When it comes to difficult people and their situations, I use a specific strategy to keep me at peace.

Imagine that you are standing outside enjoying the day when you notice a car racing down the hill. At the bottom of the hill there are people in danger of being hit by this racing car. Most people will want to do something about the situation, but they probably won't choose to jump in front of the car to stop it. We know that this car will just run us over and still hit whomever is at the bottom of the hill. The point here is that people with negative moods and destructive behaviors will eventually crash and burn with or without your input. So why even put yourself in their pathway? Next time you encounter a toxic personality, simply step out of the way and let them have their accident somewhere else. Don't become a victim of their reckless behavior.

I am not advocating waiting patiently for good things to happen in your life, or to sit back and wait for bad things to occur. I am saying that you should patiently work to increase the probability that good things will happen in your life, not only in the short duration but for the long term as well. Putting space in between your responses and actions will probably never cost you a dime; it will most certainly be the time when you overact to a situation that you will pay some kind of stiff penalty. Usually when that happens we wish we could go back and do things differently. The technique here is to always be forward thinking while putting space in between your thoughts and actions. Always look two steps ahead and weigh the risk vs. reward in every scenario or situation. From a very logical standpoint, it only makes sense to embrace iNeverWorry as the minimum standard of living because you really have nothing to lose and everything to gain.

Thank you so much for taking the time to read this book.

Your support means a lot and if anything I've said here resonates with you, please don't hesitate to share. If you want a full comprehensive training on the iNeverWorry model, you can go to our website, www.ineverworry.com, for more information.

Peace

ACKNOWLEDGMENTS

Special thanks to:

My wife, Casie Bedford, who came into my life in the midst of a storm and brought a ray of sunshine to light this path. I love you baby until the end of time.

Sandra Johnson (moms) and family, thank you for showing me seamless love and support.

My father, Donald Bedford, for showing me how to become a man in a world filled with grown boys.

My mom, LaDonna Harris, who has been showering me with love since the day she walked into my life.

My brothers, Ric Harris and Eddie Thibodeaux, for embracing me into the family.

My brother, Darrin Bedford, who is the artistic brain behind the brand and the one dude I can always count on for anything.

My cousin, John Hal Jr., who has been my sounding board and walks shoulder to shoulder with me no matter what.

My step-mom Jackie Bedford (Rest in Peace) and my sisters, Latasha Valrey and Anitra Clark, for their unconditional love and support.

My man Tony Gaskins for sharing the blueprints through his 'Birth Your Book" program and for working with me to bring his

Real Love Tour to my city.

All my beautiful children, Jazmyn, Sania, Destinee, Devin and J.R. Although I am always the one trying to inspire you all, the truth is you guys are the real inspiration to me.

My big brother, Vidal Prevost, for being a mentor and my life coach who has helped me make strategic moves along the way.

My Aunt Kat, who is more like a sister and has given me strength more times than she actually realizes.

My brother, Wesley Easter, for his ability to help me bottom line any issue when my vision gets foggy.

Judge Larry Goodman and family for believing in me when I didn't even believe in myself. You guys are the best.

Jessica Scannell, who opened the doors for my career and put together that awesome nomination for the National Spirit of Youth Award. Much love and respect.

My good friends Kesha Rae and Emillio Mena, who helped me change many lives in our community.

Andre Reynolds who still spends countless hours with me brainstorming on our next "big thing".

Rod Campbell, who gave me the insight on what it means to "Affect Culture."

To all my colleagues at the Alameda County Probation Department who have heart for this work and dedicate their lives to changing lives, one client at a time.

TT and Rashida, you both are greatly appreciated. Thanks for being a strong support system.

Tywan and Boy Wonder, thank you gentlemen for holding me up while I was busy calculating my next moves.

Mike and Nicole, my Latin connects, thanks for maintaining a unique relationship that only we understand.

Tony Crear and Sylvia Johnson (Rest in Peace), who both took a risk and gave me the opportunity to join the Department despite what the odds say about ex-felons.

To all my homeboys who lost their lives along the way and never got a chance to experience life after the streets. This one's for you, fellas. Rest in Paradise.

Ken Wilson and Todd Mayfield for covering me through the years as I made this transition from the block to the boardroom.

My sisters Stacy and Sherron Hogg, who make themselves available to me at a moment's notice and keep me grounded.

Esa Ehmen-Krause, who has not only been a great mentor and manager but an awesome friend.

Stacey Debono, who kept the feedback honest during the process and made this book submission process stress free.

Danine Manette, who showed me love and gave me valuable insight on media relations and marketing.

To all my family and friends, if you have had any type of

communication with me at all, just know you are truly appreciated. There are just way too many good folks to try and name individually.

Last but not least, a special shout out to my entire Brookfield Village family because truly, without that concrete jungle experience, I wouldn't have the game that I have today.

iNeverWorry

iNeverWorry

ABOUT THE AUTHOR

DB Bedford has been consulting and training individuals, organizations, companies and couples for the past 15 years. He has a strong passion for working with youth, families, and the community.

Being an inspiration to others and a role model to his children is of utmost importance. His goal is to leave a legacy behind so that 100 years from now the world will know that he was here.

info@ineverworry.com
www.ineverworry.com

CPSIA information can be obtained
at www.ICGtesting.com
Printed in the USA
FSHW020306061219
64812FS